Police Unarmed Defense Tactics

Third Printing

By

DONALD O. SCHULTZ, B.S., MPA

Department of Police Science
Broward Community College

CUSTOM PUBLISHING COMPANY

Copyright: © 1988 by Custom Publishing Company
ORDERS: P.O. Box 22986, Sacramento, CA 95822

Library of Congress Catalogue Number: 72-87012

ISBN 0-942728-22-X

Printed in the United States of America.

PREFACE

A LTHOUGH SCIENTIFIC DISCOVERIES and technical advances have assisted police personnel in crime detection activities, not too much has been made available to help law enforcement officers to defend themselves. Many police agencies have recently lowered requirements in the area of physical standards. This to some degree is an outgrowth of manpower shortages experienced in police departments throughout our country. The result of this trend is that while the average size of the American citizen is becoming greater, the police officer's height and weight requirements are being geared downward.

No matter what the size of the police officer, he must consider the fact that he can and will be challenged to engage in physical combat. The outcome of the conflict will depend on three basic items: (1) the officer's physical condition, (2) whether he was properly trained, (3) his mental attitude or confidence in his ability to defend himself. It is hoped that the majority of our police personnel will keep themselves in top physical condition. Towards the goal of having properly trained policemen, we can only rely on the efforts of the many fine police academies and texts written to this end.

With the attainment of good physical condition and the training to adequately defend himself in hand-to-hand combat, the street police officer can assure himself of a good confidence level.

Unarmed defense is a system of police defense and control techniques devised primarily for law enforcement officers. The techniques are relatively simple, practical and effective, and can be utilized by the officer for his self-preservation.

Objectives

In law enforcement, the individual must have physical stamina to pursue fleeing suspects, to fend off physical assaults and to adjust to unusual working conditions and schedules. Such stamina and self-confidence are achieved through proper conditioning, which is one of the main objectives of the conditioning program.

DONALD O. SCHULTZ

ACKNOWLEDGMENTS

T HE AUTHORS WISH to thank the many contributors from police agencies throughout our country. Without the assistance from these knowledgeable police personnel, this text could not have been written. We also wish to extend our appreciation to Chief Robert W. Johnston, police photographer George Tanner, Lieutenant Larry Calhoun and Charles Funkey of the Fort Lauderdale Police Department. To all those who encouraged the writing of this book and assisted with valuable information, we dedicate this text.

CONTENTS

POLICE UNARMED DEFENSE TACTICS

Third Printing

This text is written as a practical training manual to assure the police officer of an advantage while engaging in physical combat.

DONALD O. SCHULTZ, B.S., MPA

Chapter I

BASIC EXERCISES TO ATTAIN PHYSICAL FITNESS

Present-day research and development of police equipment, machines and techniques are no better than the man operating or using them. Every new advance in the speed, maneuverability, durability, communications and techniques must be accompanied by a corresponding improvement in the quality and fitness of the operators.

A close relationship exists between physical fitness, and mental and emotional fitness or morale. The mind and the body cannot be considered as separate. Fatigue, weakness, lack of stamina and physical exhaustion are usually associated with low state of health and morale. Quick thinking, evaluating, analyzing and performing should be the name of the game for every law enforcement officer.

COMPONENTS OF PHYSICAL FITNESS

Freedom from disease and defect (physiological soundness) does not in itself constitute physical fitness; it is merely the foundation upon which physical fitness is built. Before a law enforcement officer is fit for hazardous duty, good health and the absence of handicapping defects must be supplemented by strength, endurance, agility and coordination.

The human body is like a machine—the most complex, intricate and efficient machine known to man. The greater the demands and the more it is used, the more efficient it becomes. The human body improves with work while other machines simply wear out.

The key to a well-conditioned and efficient body is the cardiovascular or circulatory system comprised of the heart and blood vessels. The bloodstream carries nutrients, oxygen and hormones throughout the body, exchanging them for waste products to be eliminated.

Physical exercise properly applied, such as running, swimming, cycling and jogging, strengthens the heart, dilates the arteries, and helps maintain the elasticity of the blood vessels. The heart is a muscle and like all muscles, when organically sound, improves and becomes stronger when subjected to work.

The nature of police work today, due to mechanization and automation, causes the heart and body to deteriorate because of sedentary living and little or no exercise. On occasion, a police officer's duties may require a

3

burst of physical activity that places a tremendous strain on the heart and circulatory system that is beyond the physical capacity of the officer, resulting in physical stress and easy fatigability.

The best way to attain physical fitness is with regular participation in a number of sports. No single sport provides a truly balanced development for all parts of the body. The trend in exercise today is towards self-directed or do-it-yourself exercises, which let you develop your own pace as opposed to the old method of doing the exercise until it hurts. It is important when doing these exercises to avoid doing more than you are actually capable of doing and to maintain a regular schedule of doing the exercise each day. Self-discipline with dependable self-reliance should be the central theme for police survival.

CONDITIONING EXERCISES

Conditioning exercises constitute the most extensively used activity in a training program of unarmed defense tactics. These selected exercises have a number of advantages: (1) they can be conducted anywhere; (2) they require no equipment; (3) they are readily adaptable to large or small groups; (4) they can be easily adapted to individual physiological differences; (5) they can be regulated for quantity and progression; (6) if properly selected, they will reach and develop any desired muscle group in the body; (7) they have a carryover effect—each individual can continue the exercise at home at his own rate, speed and progression in dosage.

There are three stages in the conditioning program. The first stage lasts three weeks, during which the men through a period of muscular stiffness, soreness and recovery.

The second stage lasts from four to ten weeks, depending on the person's physical condition and age. The improvement is fairly rapid at first but becomes progressively slower.

In the third stage, the men reach a peak beyond which they appear to show little improvement. The problem here is that the individual must maintain this level on his own initiative at work or at home.

For the first two to three weeks, the number of repetitions recommended is ten to fifteen. The amount of activity is gradually increased until the tenth or twelfth week with twenty-five to thirty repetitions of each exercise representing a normal workload.

Initial Testing—Physical Profile

The following test is given in your first week in conditioning:
    Pull-ups or chinning, palms forward.
    Rope climbing—fifteen feet or better.
    Sit-ups—hands behind your head, feet held by another.

Leg lifts—legs straight.
Push-ups—body straight with no swaying or arching.
Broad jump.
One-arm push-ups.
The 220-yard run.

Conditioning Program—First Stage (Three Weeks)

The following exercises should be performed daily:

Overhand pull-ups, as many as possible; rest two minutes and then repeat three times.

Sit-ups, hands behind head—fifteen times; rest two minutes and then repeat three times.

Push-ups, hands or fists—fifteen times; two-minutes rest and repeat three times.

Jog one mile per day for five days in under eight minutes' time.

Conditioning Program—Second Stage (Four to Ten Weeks)

Repeat daily:

Overhand pull-ups, as many as possible; rest and repeat three times.

Sit-ups, hands behind head—thirty times in one minute; rest and repeat two times.

Leg lifts, legs spread and together—twenty-five times; rest one minute and repeat two times.

Push-ups, eight count—twenty-five times; one-minute rest and repeat two times.

Jog one mile per day for five days in under six minutes.

Final Evaluation

Gradual conditioning program will include physical exercises, mat work, falls, basic unarmed self-defense, supervised throws and daily one-mile runs.

At the end of your seventh week, you will be retested on the minimum physical fitness requirements. You will be considered to have made excellent progress if you can perform the following:

Seven overhand pull-ups.
Fifteen-foot rope climb.
Fifty-five sit-ups.
Forty push-ups.
220-yard run in thirty seconds or less.
One-mile run within six minutes.
7'6" broad jump.

Physical Activity for First Three Weeks

The following should be done daily:

1. *Astride jump* (2 count—20 times). Feet together, arms at side. Jump and land with feet astride and arms raised sideways to above shoulder height—overhead touching palms—keeping elbows locked. Return to start position.

2. *Body twist* (4 count—20 times). Place both hands behind head—elbows sideward. Twist body to left, then to straight position, then twist to right and then to straight position.

3. *Touch floor* (4 count—15 times). Feet astride, arms upward. Touch floor and press (bounce) once, then stretch upward and backward bend.

4. *Sit-up* (2 count—15 times). Back lying, feet six inches apart, arms at sides. Sit up to vertical position keeping feet or heels on the floor even if it is necessary to hook the toes under a chair or have the feet held by a partner for leverage.

5. *Back stretch* (2 count—15 times). Front lying, palms placed under thighs. Raise head, shoulders and both legs. Keep legs straight. Both thighs must clear the palms.

6. *Leg-lifts* (4 count—15 times). Back lying, legs straight and six inches off the ground. Lift legs overhead, then lower to six inches above ground, spread legs and return, then lift legs overhead.

7. *Push-ups* (2 count—15 times). Front lying, hands under shoulders, palms flat on the floor or clenched fist, wrist in locked position. Straight arms to lift body with only palms and toes touching the floor. Back must be kept straight and only chest must touch ground.

8. *Mile run or jogging.*

Physical Activity Fourth Week through Tenth Week

Listed below are the activities to do.

1. *Astride jump* (2 count—30 times).

2. *Body twist* (2 count—30 times).

3. *Touch floor, bend and reach* (5 count—30 times). Side straddle, arms on hips. Bend trunk forward, touch floor and press bounce twice, then swing arms backward between the legs, palms down, and touch fingers to ground between and behind the heels. Knees are bent. Touch fingers as far behind heels as possible. Do not raise heels. Recover to starting position, arms on hips and backward bend. Recover to starting position and repeat exercise count (1).

4. *Sit-up* Touching knees with opposite elbow (4 count—30 times). Back lying, feet six inches apart, fingers laced behind head, elbows backward. Sit up to verticle position. Bend forward, touching your left knee

with the right elbow and return to start position. Lying on back, sit up to verticle position, bend forward touching right knee with the left elbow. Repeat exercise. Alternate exercise is to raise both knees toward chest and touch each knee with the opposite elbow.

5. *Body twist* (4 count—25 times). Position on back, arms on ground and extend sideward, palms down, legs nearly verticle, feet together, knees straight. Lower legs to the left, twisting trunk and touching ground next to left hand, keeping knees straight and both shoulders on the ground. Legs must be lowered, not dropped. Recover to starting position without bending knees. Lower legs to right, twisting trunk and touching ground near right hand. Recover to starting position.

6. *Leg lifts, spread and together* (4 count—25 times).

7. *Eight-count push-up* (8 count—25 times). Starting position of attention.

    A. Bend at knees and hips and place hands on floor in front of feet in squatting position.

    B. Thrust feet and legs backward to front-leaning rest position. Keep body straight from head to heels. Support weight on hands and toes.

    C. Bend elbows and touch chest to ground.

    D. Recover to front-leaning position.

    E. Bend elbows and touch chest to ground.

    F. Recover to front-leaning position.

    G. Recover to squatting position

    H. Recover to starting position.

8. *Mile run or jogging* (6 minutes). Running is an excellent conditioning activity for developing muscular endurance and increased efficiency in the functioning of the heart, vascular system and the lungs. It is recommended that running be an every day activity.

9. *Stationary run* (2 minutes). (Alternate for mile run or jogging for indoors.) Start standing with arms in loose thrust position. Start slow, then fast, then slow. Begin run slowly, then speed up, raising the knees above the hip level. Increase speed gradually to full speed, raise knees hard, then slow down. For persons in good condition, this exercise should continue for approximately two minutes. The middle portion of time should be at top speed.

Chapter II

BASIC PRINCIPLES

Balance

BALANCE IS PROBABLY the most important principle in the execution of any physical skill. In balanced position, a person can utilize his full physical potential. Maintaining a good balanced position requires a moderate spread of the feet, staggering them by placing the right foot slightly ahead of the left, and lowering the center of gravity by bending the knees a little and lowering the buttocks.

Good Body Mechanics

TRUNK MUSCLES. Develop the use of proper muscles in the proper way at the proper time. The large trunk muscles, particularly the abdominal and oblique muscle, play an important part in many physical movements. When in good condition or tone, these muscles are loaded with power, and when they are properly used, your physical capabilities are greatly increased.

BREATH CONTROL. Breath control is important because when you inhale, your abdominal muscles are relaxed; if you exhale sharply, the abdominal muscles become tense. By holding the breath, you "set" your diaphragm, thus minimizing the effectiveness of a blow to the chest or abdomen.

Leverage

The human body contains a great many levers. Knowing where and how to apply leverage increases your chances in overcoming and controlling a stronger opponent.

Strength against Weakness

The human body has many weak or vulnerable areas. The objective is to direct all of your strength and power toward your opponent's weakness or vulnerable area.

Using Opponent's Strength and Momentum to His Disadvantage

"PUSH-PULL PRINCIPLE." When the opponent pushes you, rather than resisting or bracing up and pushing back, go with the hold or pull him toward you as he pushes, thus breaking his balance momentarily and making the opponent move forward with little or no control. Go with the hold rather than resist him directly. Use your strength and power to guide and direct his movements.

Chapter III

FUNDAMENTALS

The Combat Stance

T HIS IS THE STANCE used by the police officer defending himself when being attacked (Fig. 1). The feet should be spread a little wider than the shoulders. Feet should be staggered, the right foot slightly forward and the left foot slightly to the rear. The knees should be bent, the buttocks lowered and the weight evenly distributed on the balls of the feet. Hands should be held about chest or face high, and the arms and elbows reasonably close to the body. This is a strong balanced position and should be assumed to meet the attack.

Figure 1. Combat stance.   Figure 2. Footwork.

Once attacked, the stance is similar to a fighting stance (Fig. 2). One foot should be forward and one foot backward, the lead foot bent at the knee 45 degrees, and about 40 to 60 percent of the body weight on the forward foot. The back foot should be straight, heel flat on the ground. The fists should be clenched and elbows close to the body. Most blows are directed to the head, the solar plexus or stomach areas. The lead hand goes forward and the opposite hand is snapped rapidly backward. All body muscles tighten at the moment of impact. Exhale, and deliver the blow from a solid stance.

Footwork

Movement involving the feet should be done in such a manner as to constantly maintain a strong, balanced position. Keep the feet close to the floor. The first foot to move should be the foot nearest the direction you wish to go. Avoid crossing the feet. The lead foot leads us forward and to the side. The rear leads us backward and to that side (Fig. 2).

Alert Defensive Stance

This stance should be used when you are talking to a suspect or subject (Fig. 3). Stand a little more than arm's length from the individual, facing him at about a 45-degree angle with your gun side away from the subject. The feet should be reasonably spread and staggered, the knees slightly bent and the hands held chest high. This position allows you to go into action quickly in defending yourself against an attack (Fig. 4), yet it does not arouse suspicion or antagonize the suspect.

Figures 3 and 4. Alert defensive stance.

Personal Weapons

These are parts of the body which can be used for self-defense and counterattack. Developing skill in the use of your personal weapons should enable you to defend yourself successfully when attacked.

THE HEAD. The front (Fig. 5) and back (Fig. 6) of the head can be used for butting.

THE HAND. The wrist should be held straight for all blows (Fig. 7) except the "heel-of-hand" blow (Fig. 8) which is delivered upward when you are close to your opponent. The "edge-of-hand" (Fig. 9) and the "edge-of-fist" (Fig. 10) blows are most effective when delivered with a chopping motion across the body. Blows delivered from across the body permit the use of the large trunk muscles. When used correctly, these muscles add considerable speed and force to the blow.

The heel-of-hand (Fig. 8) blow is delivered upward when you are close to your opponent. In the "finger jab" (Fig. 9), the finger must be flexed

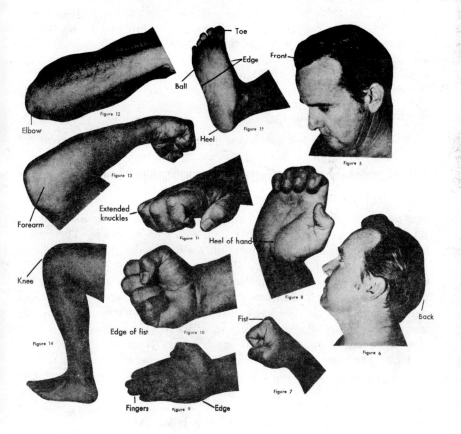

slightly and held rigid. The "extended knuckles" (Fig. 11) blow requires the thumb to be held firmly against the index finger and the wrist to be in a straight-locked position, thus giving the hand a firm position.

THE ELBOWS. The elbow should be fully flexed when used as a weapon (Fig. 12). This is probably the most powerful blow the average person can deliver and the most effective when delivered to the rear. A forearm (Fig. 13) or elbow blow can be thrown by raising the arm shoulder high, flexing the elbow, then swinging the arm forward toward the side or straight upward from the waist.

THE KNEE. "Knee lifts" to the body's vulnerable areas or to the groin can be very effective when properly performed. The knee should be flexed fully by pulling the foot back as close to the buttocks as possible as the knee is raised (Fig. 14). The knee lift and other kicks must be executed quickly and then immediately returned to a strong balanced position.

THE FOOT. (See Fig. 15.) The ball of the foot is used in kicking forward; the edge, ball and heel are used in kicking sideward and backward. The heel is used in stamping. To execute a kick properly, first flex the hip and then raise the knee until the thigh is parallel to the floor. The lower leg is then "snapped" or thrust" out to complete the kick. A short snappy kick is extremely effective when directed against the opponent's groin, knee, shin or other vulnerable areas of the body.

Vulnerable Areas of the Body

The human body has many vulnerable spots. Some of these areas are nerve centers, some are organs unprotected by a bony or muscular structure, some are areas only lightly protected by a bony or muscular structure and some are areas only lightly protected by a bone or muscle tissue. A well-timed blow by the hand, fist, fingers, knee or foot, or pressure brought to bear on one of these vital areas will disable an opponent or force him to cease offensive action or completely incapacitate an opponent. These spots are listed in the order of their vulnerability and accessibility.

TESTICLES. These organs are the most sensitive and vulnerable of a man's body. A blow to the groin with the hand, foot or knee will disable the strongest opponent. The strongest of holds can be broken if the testicles can be grasped or hit. Because of their vulnerable location, they are the most likely spot at which to expect an attack from an opponent. A knee blow to the testicle area usually terminates any resistance.

EYES. The eyes are very delicate and easy to reach. Man instinctively tries to protect his eyes, and a gouge to the eye with the thumb or finger will be effective in breaking the most determined hold or attack. A blow which is aimed or feinted at the eyes will cause a man to instinctively cover them and he may leave himself open to other types of attack.

NECK AREA. A blow with the edge of the hand across the windpipe in the "Adam's apple" can have a fatal effect. A strong blow of this type will result in crushing the windpipe.

Blows delivered by the edge of the hand to the sides of the throat and the back of the neck at the base of the skull have a knockout effect. Blows delivered lightly to the sides and the back of the neck with the edge of the hand or fist will demonstrate their effectiveness clearly.

BACK AND KIDNEY AREA. The main muscle cords and nerves of the body branch out from the base of the spine at a point very near the surface. This area is commonly known as the small of the back. The kidneys are located in this area just above the hips on each side of the spine. A horizontal blow with the edge of the hand or fist, or a kick in this area will have a disabling or possibly a knockout effect. The blow must be delivered above the hipbones and below the heavy back muscles.

A low blow with the edge of the hand to the end of the spine is often effective and is easiest to deliver when the opponent is stooping over as he would be if grappling someone about the waist. A kick delivered by the point of the toe to this area often produces a disabling effect.

ABDOMINAL AREA. A hard blow delivered to the abdominal area by the fist, knee or head is very effective, particularly if the opponent's muscles are relaxed. The solar plexus can be hit by driving the fist up under the rib structure at a point just above the navel.

CHIN. A knockout effect can be produced by a blow with the heel of the hand given to the point of the opponent's chin. A blow with the edge of the hand, directed downward at the point of the chin will dislocate or break the lower jawbone.

NOSE. A horizontal blow with the edge of the hand at that part of the nose usually covered by the bridge of a pair of glasses will result in a knockout and possibly death. A blow to this area of the nose may result in crushing of the most fragile bones of the facial structure. Another vulnerable spot is reached by placing the index fingers on both sides of the nose at its base where it joins the face and pressing inward and upward. An upward blow with the edge of the hand at the base of the nose is also very effective.

TEMPLES. A blow delivered to the temple area with the knuckles or the edge of the hand will often result in a knockout. This small area is one of the most sensitive on the head. This vulnerable area can be located by placing the thumbs on the temples and exerting a firm, steady, inward pressure.

SIDE OF THE HEAD. At a point back of the ears and at the base of the head, a blow with the back of the fist or hand or the edge of the hand with a snapping motion can be very devastating.

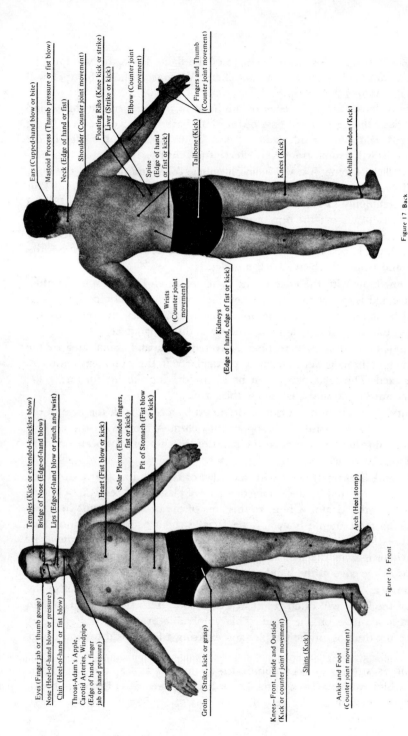

Eyes (Finger jab or thumb gouge)
Nose (Heel-of-hand blow or pressure)
Chin (Heel-of-hand or fist blow)
Throat—Adam's Apple,
Carotid Arteries, Windpipe
(Edge of hand, finger
jab or hand pressure)

Temples (Kick or extended-knuckles blow)
Bridge of Nose (Edge-of-hand blow)
Lips (Edge-of-hand blow or pinch and twist)

Heart (Fist blow or kick)
Solar Plexus (Extended fingers, fist or kick)
Pit of Stomach (Fist blow or kick)

Groin (Strike, kick or grasp)

Knees—Front, Inside and Outside
(Kick or counter joint movement)

Shins (Kick)

Ankle and Foot
(Counter joint movement)

Arch (Heel stomp)

Figure 16 Front

Ears (Cupped-hand blow or bite)
Mastoid Process (Thumb pressure or fist blow)
Neck (Edge of hand or fist)
Shoulder (Counter joint movement)
Floating Ribs (Knee kick or strike)
Liver (Strike or kick)
Elbow (Counter joint movement)
Fingers and Thumb
(Counter joint movement)

Spine
(Edge of hand
or fist or kick)
Tailbone (Kick)
Kidneys
(Edge of hand, edge of fist or kick)
Wrists
(Counter joint
movement)
Knees (Kick)
Achilles Tendon (Kick)

Figure 17 Back

16

JAW-HINGE AREA. The point near the ears where the lower jaw is hinged to the upper is a very sensitive area vulnerable to a knuckle blow. This area can be located by placing the fingertips just under the earlobe and pressing in and up. An opponent will quickly stop offensive action or will release a hold if pressure is applied at these points.

JOINTS. Joints of the knee, wrist, elbow, arm, fingers and other members of the body are designed to bend in only one direction. Strong blows or pressure in the opposite direction applied to these joints will force an opponent to yield and will possibly break or dislocate the joint.

SENSITIVE BONES. Many bones which are not covered with protective flesh or tissue are very sensitive to blows. Kicks or blows with the edge of the hand to the collarbone, forearm or wrist will often cause the opponent to release his hold and may result in a break to the bone. Grips by an opponent may be broken by forcing a knuckle or the point of your thumb between the small bones at the back of the opponent's hand. The soft area where the tumb joins the hand is also very sensitive to this type of pressure.

OTHER SENSITIVE AREAS. The following actions are very effective in breaking grips and created openings: pulling the hair, tearing a lip, grasping and twisting the nose, kicking the Achilles tendon at the back of the heel and gripping or pinching the thick muscles close to the neck that extend from the neck to the shoulder.

Chapter IV

PRACTICE FALL POSITIONS

Y OU MUST FIRST LEARN various fall positions before you attempt the throws that are taught in unarmed defense tactics. Physical conditioning and constant practice in these positions will enable you to be thrown with less chance of being injured.

Side Break Fall from Forward Roll

RIGHT SIDE FALL. Start from the standing position and raise your left arm over your head with the palm of your hand facing to the left. Take several steps forward to build up momentum. When your left foot strikes the ground, swing your raised left arm down in an arc through your legs so that you go into a forward somersault. Keep your chin tucked into your chest. At the peak of your forward roll, thrust your flexed legs so that your body is propelled into the air feetfirst and parallel to the ground in an extended position. The sole of your left foot and the palm of your right hand are driven to the ground and make the initial contact which absorbs most of the shock. The completed fall position should be the same as in Figure 18.

LEFT SIDE FALL. The left side fall position can be practiced in a similar manner. An alternate method would be the left hand placed on the ground

Figure 18. Right side break fall.

19

or mat, the right hand placed on the stomach, palm in, the right foot placed forward and the left foot backward (Fig. 19). Go into a forward roll with your right foot being driven to the ground, your left arm slamming with palm down. Your right arm is in the "on-guard" position (Fig. 20).

Figure 19. Left side break fall—start.

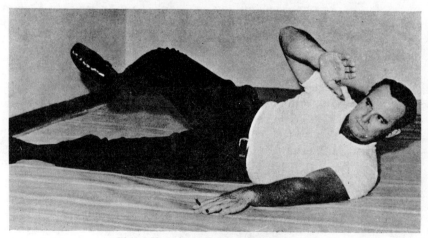

Figure 20. Left side break fall—completed.

Points to check for the right side fall position are as follows:

1. Your left foot is driven to the ground, and takes up the initial shock of the fall. It strikes the ground behind your right leg at the knee. The sole of your foot is flat on the ground.

2. Your right arm is the "slamming" arm and takes up additional shock. It is extended along the ground, palm down with fingers extended and joined, at an angle of 45 degrees to the body. This arm makes contact with the ground at the same time as your left foot.

3. Your chin is tucked into your chest, keeping your head off the ground. Your neck remains tense to prevent your head from striking the ground and being injured.

4. The entire right side of your body makes solid contact with the ground. To prevent your right leg from being injured, relax it by bending it slightly at the knee.

5. Your left hand is bent and in the on-guard position to prevent any attack against the face, head or chest.

Squat Position Break Fall

FORWARD ROLL. Starting position (Fig. 21) : assume the squatting position and place your hands between your knees with the palms flat on the ground and fingers pointing toward each other. Roll forward in a somersault (Fig. 22). At the peak of the forward roll, arch your back and tuck your chin into your chest to keep your head from striking the ground. Drive the soles of the feet to the ground about shoulder width apart and simultaneously slap both hands to the ground. The arms are fully extended with the hands palm down forming a 45-degree angle to your body. The completed fall should be the same as in Figure 23.

Points to check for in the forward roll are as follow:

1. The soles of your feet are driven to the ground about shoulder width apart, keeping your lower legs at a 90-degree angle to the ground. This takes up the initial shock of the fall.

2. Both hands strike the ground in a slapping motion at the same time as your feet. The arms are fully extended, forming a 45-degree angle to your body and the palms of your hands are down. This slapping motion gives you contact with the ground with both arms and shoulders taking up additional shock.

3. Keep your stomach muscles tighented so your buttocks will not strike the ground when you land. This prevents injury to your spine.

4. Your chin is tucked into your chest so that your head does not strike the ground.

BACKWARD ROLL. Starting position (Fig. 24) : assume the squatting position and place your arms in a crossed position in front of your chest. Roll backwards and tuck your chin into your chest to keep your head from striking the ground (Fig. 25). At the peak of the backward roll, shoulders hit the ground and simultaneously both hands are slapped to the ground. The

Figures 21 and 22. Squat position break fall—forward roll.

arms are fully extended with the hands palm down forming a 45-degree angle to your body. Completed fall should be the same as in Figure 26.

Side Break Fall from Standing Position

In the standing position, the arms are crossed at the chest level, weight is shifted to the left foot as the right foot is swept forward and upward to the left (Fig. 27). With a slight lift off the ground with the aid of the left foot, the fall to the ground is on the right side. Your left foot is driven to the ground, taking up the shock of the fall. The sole of the foot is flat on

Figure 23. Squat position break fall—forward roll.

the ground. Your right arm is slammed to the ground and takes additional shock. The arm is extended along the ground, palm down, with fingers extended and at an angle of 45-degrees to the body. This arm makes contact with the ground at the same time as your left foot. Your chin is tucked into your chest, with the neck tense to prevent your head from striking the ground and being injured. Your left arm is held across your face and head for protection from the blows of your opponent. The entire right side of your body makes solid contact with the ground (Fig. 28).

Side Break Fall from Roll-off

Starting position is with the subject on his hands and knees, his body parallel to the ground (Fig. 29). With your right hand, grasp hold of the shirt over the subject's left shoulder. Bend your right arm close to your body and place your right shoulder on top and over his right shoulder (Fig. 30). Your right hip is over his right hip. Roll off his back. The entire left side of your body makes solid contact with the ground. To prevent your left leg from being injured, relax it by bending it slight at the knee. Your left foot takes part of the shock of the fall. The left arm takes up the additional shock of the fall. The arm is extended along the ground, palm down, fingers extended and joined together at an angle of 45-degrees to the body. Your chin is tucked into your chest and the neck is tense (Fig. 31).

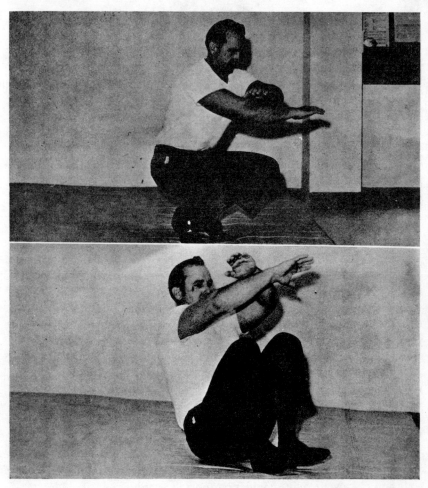

Figures 24 and 25. Squat position break fall—backward roll.

Figures 26. Squat position break fall—backward roll.

Figures 27 and 28. Side break fall from standing position.

Figures 29 and 30. Side break fall from roll-off.

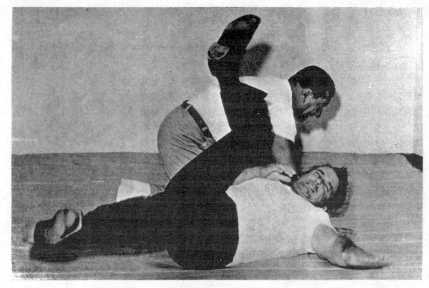

Figure 31. Side break fall from roll-off.

Chapter V

COME-ALONG HOLDS

COME-ALONG HOLDS are usually used to escort individuals for short distances. The handcuffs should be used to control the subject for long distances.

When approaching a suspect opponent, maintain a sideway stance with your nearest foot forward to block any blows to the groin. *Always* keep your gun side away from the person you are interviewing or approaching.

Your first point of contact from a sideway approach should be the suspect or opponent's upper arm just above the elbow to prevent a sudden blow to your groin or other part of your body.

Select one or two favorite come-along holds and practice.

Original Thumb and Forefinger Come-along Hold

Opponent is standing slightly to your right and facing you.

Step in with your right foot and grasp opponent's right hand with your right hand, turning your hand over so that your thumb is on the back of his hand. Your fingers are curled around the little finger side of his hand and into his palm (Fig. 32). Bend his hand toward him as you raise his arm shoulder high. Place your left thumb against the back of his hand with your fingers around the base of his thumb and into his palm. Bend his wrist toward him and roll it forward, keeping his arm straight as you move out to the side and toward his head (Fig. 33). Maintain pressure on his wrist as you encircle his thumb and forefinger with the thumb and forefinger of your left hand. Release your right hand, slide upward along his arm and grasp his right arm above his elbow as you take his hand clockwise toward his body. Continue passing his hand around next to his body, touching his fingers up against his armpit. When his hand is in front of his armpit, pull his elbow into your left armpit and hold his arm firmly between your left arm and body. Pain is inflicted by forcing his hand back toward him and then twisting it outward or toward you (Fig. 34). To be an effective come-along hold, the palm of your hand should cover the back of his hand.

Enough pressure should be applied to keep the suspect walking on his tiptoes. The thumb and forefinger come-along is an effective technique used to move resisting suspects a short distance. This hold is particularly useful in handling female suspects. No permanent damage is done by twisting the wrist and the officer appears to be helping the person along.

27

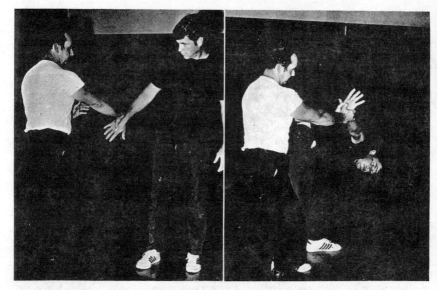

Figures 32 and 33. Original thumb and forefinger come-along.

Figure 34. Original thumb and forefinger come-along.

Original Bent Wrist

Approach the opponent from his right side. Your nearest leg should be first and forward to avoid a blow to your groin. With your left hand, grasp his right arm above the elbow, your thumb on the inside of the wrist with palm and fingers across the back of his hand. Bend opponent's wrist back with your right hand as you raise his forearm parallel to the floor (Fig. 35). Move in close to him as you push his elbow under your armpit and grasp his four fingers with your left hand. Your palm should be on top of the back of his hand and your thumb underneath the bend of his right wrist (Fig. 36). *Note*: His elbow must be held securely between your left arm and body directly below your armpit. Your thumbs should be under his wrist joint.

Figures 35 and 36. Original bent wrist.

Fingerlock

Approach opponent from the side, your closest foot guarding you from a blow to the groin. Grasp the opponent's arm above the elbow with your left hand; your right hand grasps the opponent's index or middle finger. Grasp the fingers as close to his hand as possible and squeeze them together (Fig. 37). With a snapping motion, twist his palm upward as you hold his elbow steady with your left hand (Fig. 38). Move in beside him and strike an edge-of-hand blow with your left hand inside and at the break of his

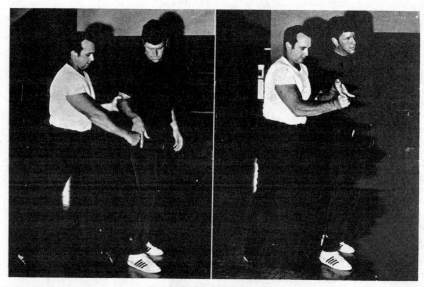

Figures 37 and 38. Fingerlock.

Figure 39. Fingerlock.

elbow as you bend his fingers back, forcing his elbow back and pinning it between your left arm and body. Now reach forward with your left hand and grasp his two middle fingers close to his hand and release your right hand. You can now control him with just your left hand by bending his fingers back and twisting them under and up toward him (Fig. 39). *Note:* His left elbow must be held securely between your left arm and body directly below your armpit.

Bar Hammerlock

FROM THE FRONT. You are standing facing your opponent and slightly toward his right. Step forward with your right foot and place the outside of your right wrist against opponent's left forearm near his wrist. Force his arm slightly backward and away from his body. At the same time, use your left hand to grasp the back of his arm directly above the elbow (biceps) (Fig. 40). Immediately roll his arm forward and downward with your left hand as you force his forearm to the rear with your right wrist causing his elbow to bend. Now move behind him as you drive your left hand above his elbow, catching his wrist in the crotch of your elbow (Fig. 41). You should now be behind him and slightly toward his left side. Now place your right forearm next to his back and bring your right shoulder close to his back to prevent his wrist from slipping out from the crotch of your elbow. To maintain better control, lift your right elbow upward as you exert pressure downward on his elbow with your right hand. The opponent will have a tendency to turn toward you. To prevent this, grasp clothing above his left shoulder with your left hand and straighten him up (Fig. 42), or hook him under the chin with your left cupped hand to straighten him up. By exerting pressure as you twist to the left and moving your left foot to the rear, you can spin opponent to the left and take him to the floor either on his head and knees or flat on his stomach (Fig. 43).

Note: Attempting to "shortcut" this technique by passing your right arm inside his left arm and curling your hand up over his elbow places you in a vulnerable position. Your opponent may trap your arm by grasping his left hand with his right and exerting pressure forward and upward.

FROM THE SIDE. You are behind your opponent and to the right side, both facing the same direction. Approach the opponent by placing your nearest or left leg first to protect yourself from a blow to the groin. With your left hand, grasp the opponent's right arm above the elbow. Grasp opponent's right wrist with your right hand (Fig. 44). With the heel of your hand (fingers and thumb up), lift his right arm upward and rotate clockwise, keeping your left elbow low so that his forearm will pass over your forearm (Fig. 45). Trap his wrist in the crotch of your left elbow as you move in close and follow with the action depicted in Figure 46. Exerting downward pressure on opponent's right elbow, take him to the floor flat on his stomach for handcuffing procedure (Fig. 47).

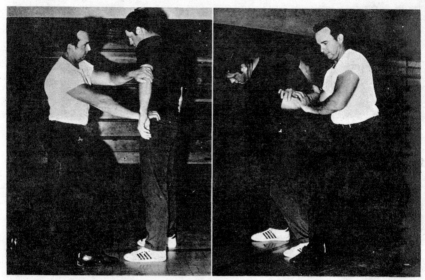

Figures 40 and 41. Bar hammerlock—from front.

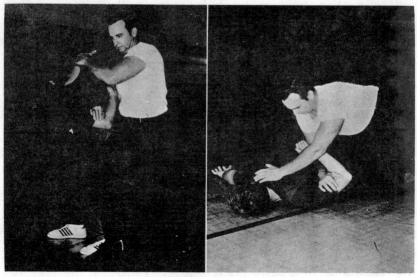

Figures 42 and 43. Bar hammerlock—from front.

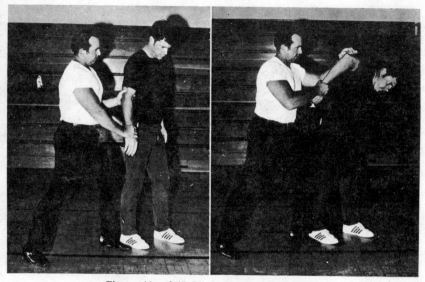

Figures 44 and 45. Bar hammerlock—from side.

Figure 46. Bar hammerlock—from side.

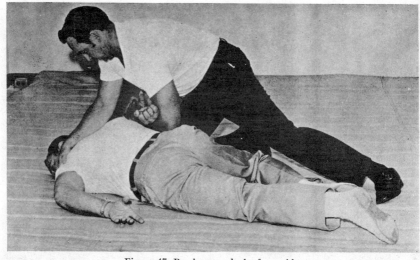

Figure 47. Bar hammerlock—from side.

Chapter VI

SELF-DEFENSE TECHNIQUES

A s POLICE officers, we are frequently called upon to arrest persons who are unwilling to be taken into custody and who offer some degree of physical resistance. When this occurs, we must be physically capable of effecting their arrest as quickly and humanely as possible. We must be familiar with those unarmed defense tactics and arrest techniques which will enable us to accomplish the arrest with a minimum of danger to ourselves and the person being arrested.

Unarmed defense tactics are simply physical techniques intended for use when weapons are not available or their use is inappropriate or inadvisable. As police officers, we are equipped with a variety of weapons but we cannot rely solely upon them; frequently, the nature of the incident in which we become involved does not permit the use of weapons.

Relatively simple, effective and easy-to-remember holds, throws and other tactics are much more practical and important to us than detailed and complicated procedures which are easily forgotten when not practiced or utilized frequently. The extent to which these techniques will be applied depends on the situations encountered. In unusual situations, it may be necessary to resort to offensive techniques as the only means of effecting an arrest, while in other situations only simple restraints and defensive techniques may be necessary. Good judgment is extremely important in deciding which tactical maneuvers will be used and how much force will be applied. We must bear in mind that the tactics used can cause injury to the person being arrested and that any force used must be reasonable and necessary under the circumstances.

Defense against Wrist and Arm Holds

ONE-HANDED GRASP ON WRIST. Maintain a strong, balanced position with your right foot forward. Either step in toward your opponent or pull him toward you so that your arm is flexed and close to your body (Fig. 48). First fake downward and against his finger grip (the strong side), then immediately pull your right forearm to the left and across your body, twisting your forearm in the direction of the area where your opponent's fingers and thumb meet (the weak side) (Fig. 49). Counter with the edge-of-fist or back-of-fist blow to the base of the head behind opponent's left ear or other vulnerable area (Fig. 50).

Figures 48 and 49. One-handed grasp on wrist.

Figure 50. One-handed grasp on wrist.

Two-Handed Grasp On Wrist. Maintain a strong, balanced position with your right foot forward. Your right arm should be flexed and close to your body. Immediately place your left arm between his forearms and grasp your right fist with your left hand (Fig. 51). Continue twisting the trunk and pulling the right arm across your body until you are free (Fig. 52). Counter with an elbow blow or an edge-of-fist or back-of-fist blow to the jaw, the side of the head or the solar plexus (Fig. 53).

Grasp On Upper Arm. Opponent grabs your right upper arm with his left hand, thumb to the inside and over the biceps muscle (Fig. 54). Throw your right hand behind, up and over opponent's left arm. Quickly bring your right fist in tight to your right shoulder, trapping opponent's left hand between your forearm and upper arm (Fig. 55). Immediately grasp your right fist with the left hand and pull your right arm down sharply and across your body, applying pressure to opponent's wrist and thereby disturbing his balance (Fig. 56). When opponent's balance has been broken, you can release your left hand and deliver a blow.

Defense against Body Lock Waist Holds

Body Lock From Front, Arms Pinned. Opponent grasps you around the body from the front (bear hug); your arms are pinned to your sides (Fig. 57). Immediately spread your feet as you bend your knees and lower the buttocks. This is a strong, balanced position with a low center of gravity and a wide base of support. With both fists, butt into the opponent's groin, jabbing his abdomen with your thumbs, or use a knee lift to the groin (Fig. 58). Place your left hand on top of his right shoulder and your right hand on opponent's back left hip area (Fig. 59). Pivot and place your hips under opponent and throw him to the floor (Fig 60).

Body Lock From Rear, Arms Pinned. Opponent grasps you around the body from rear, your arms pinned (Fig. 61). Immediately widen your feet as you bend the knees and lower the buttocks, thus assuming a strong, balanced position with a low center of gravity and a wide base of support. You can now butt him in the face with the back of your head; move your hips slightly forward and sideward and strike a hand blow backward into his groin; exert strong pressure forward with your upper arms against his forearms and then quickly deliver an elbow blow backward into his torso or stamp down on his foot with your heel. After loosening his grasp, place your left hand just above his left knee to maintain your balance and at the same time, twist to your left and move your left leg to the rear, placing it behind his right foot (Fig. 62). Arch your body slightly back, throwing him off balance. You can now throw him to the ground by turning your head toward him as you sweep him backward with your left arm and shoulder, pick up both of his legs at the knees and dump him backward (Fig. 63).

Figures 51 and 52. Two-handed grasp on wrist.

Figure 53. Two-handed grasp on wrist.

Figures 54 and 55. Grasp on upper arm.

Figure 56. Grasp on upper arm.

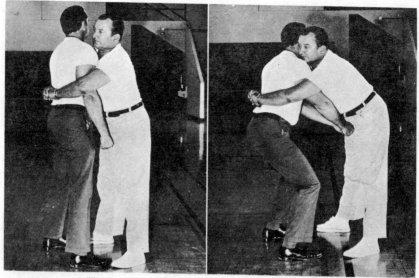

Figures 57 and 58. Body lock from front, arms pinned.

Figures 59 and 60. Body lock from front, arms pinned.

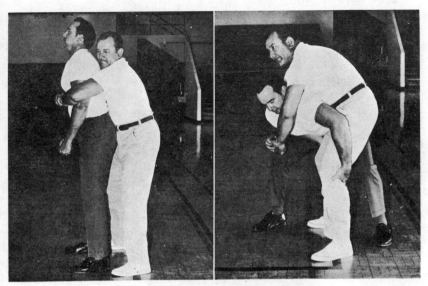

Figures 61 and 62. Body lock rear, arms pinned.

Figure 63. Body lock from rear, arms pinned.

ALTERNATE METHOD—WAIST HOLD FROM REAR, ARMS PINNED. Expand your chest and shoot both arms forward; at the same time, bend at the waist and butt opponent in the stomach area with your buttocks (Fig. 64). Bending forward and reaching between your legs, seize opponent's right or left ankle with both hands and pull it forward and upward while keeping your buttocks pressured on his kneecap or thigh.

Figure 64. Alternate method—waist hold from rear, arms pinned.

Defense against Head Holds

HEADLOCK. Opponent has a headlock and is attempting to twist you down to the ground (Fig. 65). Immediately spread your feet, bend knees and lower your center of gravity. Place your left foot well forward, and behind opponent's feet. Place your left hand under his chin or nose, forcing his head up and backward, and then deliver a right-hand blow to his groin or abdomen (Fig. 66).

As an alternate method, you can work your left shoulder and arm in front of the opponent's body. With both feet in position as above, you arch backward, placing your opponent off balance (Fig. 67). Place your left hand under opponent's left knee and your right hand under his right knee, lifting both legs up and falling backwards on opponent's head and shoulders (Fig. 68).

Figures 65 and 66. Headlock.

Figures 67 and 68. Headlock.

Defense against Kicks

Counter To Standing Kick From Front. Opponent is facing you and attempts to kick your groin or midsection with his right foot (Fig. 69). From your combat stance, clench your fists tightly, arms close to your body, and cross your forearms as you step in with your left foot bent, body straight. Block the kick with the "V" formed by your crossed arms in a forward thrust, arms extended (Fig. 70). The block should be made on the foot, ankle or lower leg. After blocking, open your hands to grasp his foot and jerk it upward, lifting the leg upward as you push him backward to the floor.

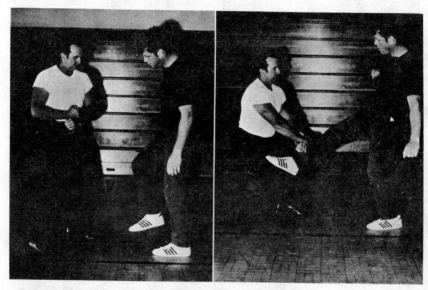

Figures 69 and 70. Defense against kicks from front.

Defense against Choke Holds

Counter To Choke From Front, Arms Extended—Using The Slap-Of-The-Wrist Technique. Opponent attempts to strangle you from the front by grasping your throat with both of his hands, arms extended. Maintain a balanced position with feet shoulder width apart, knees slightly bent. With the heel of your right hand, strike inside his right wrist. Extending your right arm full length (Fig. 71), reverse your body movement to the right and strike inside his left wrist with the heel of your left hand, extending your left arm full length (Fig. 72). Counter with your punch to the stomach or solar plexus (Fig. 73).

Figures 71 and 72. Slap on wrist.

Figure 73. Slap on wrist.

COUNTER TO CHOKE FROM FRONT, ARMS EXTENDED—USING WEDGE TECHNIQUE. Opponent attempts to strangle you from the front by grasping your throat with both of his hands, arms extended. Clasp your hands together close to your body as you bend your knees (Fig. 74). Form a wedge with your hands and drive the hands sharply upwards inside opponent's arms and as close to his hands as possible as you extend both legs and explode upward (Fig. 75). From this position, smash your clasped hands in a downward blow to opponent's bridge of the nose, face or collarbone (Fig. 76). *Caution:* Do not interlock fingers, as the counter blow may damage your fingers.

COUNTER TO CHOKE FROM REAR, ARMS EXTENDED. In starting position depicted in Figure 77, turn backward toward your opponent with a windmill motion of the right arm over both the opponent's arms and lock above the elbows. Pivot from outside and backward, locking both arms with your right hand and using the other hand to apply a punch to the stomach or the side of the body (Fig. 78).

COUNTER TO CHOKE FROM THE REAR—CLOSE UP. An opponent may attack you from the rear with a one-arm strangle or choke hold (Fig. 79). Reach up with your left hand and grab his right forearm. Pull on his forearm and at the same time tuck your chin into your chest so he cannot choke you. Grab your opponent's right shoulder with your right hand, your feet shoulder width apart, knees slightly bent and body lowered. Drive your buttocks against his midsection, retaining your hold on his forearm and shoulder with both hands (Fig. 80). By bending from the waist and straightening your legs swiftly, you can throw your opponent over your head (Fig. 81). Continue your movement, throwing your opponent to the ground (Fig. 82). As your opponent hits the ground, strike at a vulnerable point.

COUNTER TO CHOKE FROM FRONT, ARMS EXTENDED—OVERHEAD THROW USING LEG TOSS. In start position, you are facing your opponent as he is choking you from the front, his arms extended. Reach with both of your arms inside his extended arms and grasp his clothing at the chest or upper shoulder area (Fig. 83). Pull him forward as you sit down suddenly, roll backward, and place your right foot into his lower abdomen, the knee bent (Fig. 84). Your leg is then extended forcefully, causing your opponent to be thrown over your head (Fig. 85). The result of this throw is the reduction of your opponent's momentum. Final position of opponent is depicted in Figure 86.

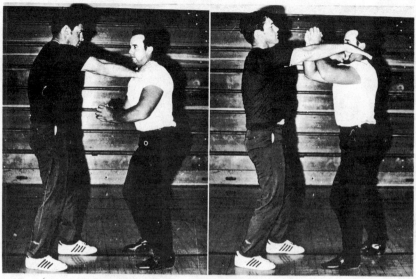

Figures 74 and 75. Counter to choke from front—wedge.

Figure 76. Counter to choke from front—wedge.

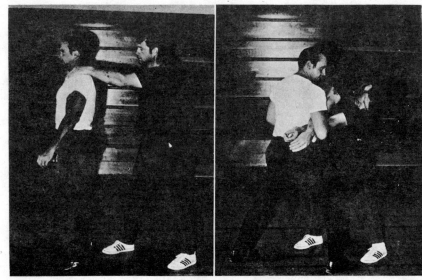

Figures 77 and 78. Counter to choke from rear, arms extended.

Defense against a roundhouse Punch to the Face

FLYING MARE. Opponent throws right-handed roundhouse punch to the face (Fig. 87). Facing your opponent, block his right hand with your left hand, making first contact with his right wrist (Fig. 88), and grasping it. Place your left toe in front of his left toe and pivot to the left by putting the right toe in front of his right toe. Grasp upper portion of opponent's arm with your right hand. Turn your back to the opponent rapidly, and place your right shoulder under his right armpit (Fig. 89). Spread your feet shoulder width, bend them slightly, and throw him over your head by a quick bend at the hips (Fig. 90).

A variation of the "flying mare" is the use of the knee bend in which you secure the arm firmly over your shoulder, then drop to one knee, bend quickly forward, and throw opponent over your head to the ground (Fig. 91).

Defense against Push on Chest

Opponent places his left hand on your chest in an effort to push you backward. Place your outside hand (the elbow side) over your opponent's hand close to his wrist and hold it tight against your chest. The left hand is placed over your right hand (Fig. 92). Exert pressure on his wrist, and

Figures 79 and 80. Counter to choke from rear—close-up.

Figure 81. Counter to choke from rear—close-up.

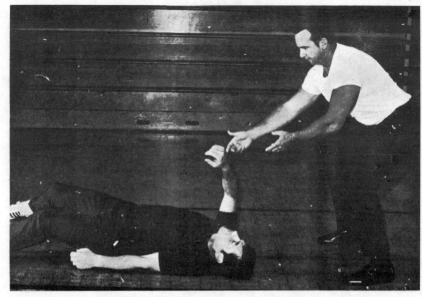

Figure 82. Counter to choke from rear—close-up.

cause him to bend forward as you bend your trunk slightly forward and twist to your left (Fig. 93). Counter with your left elbow to the chest or left knee to the chest area (Fig. 94).

Defense against Grasp on Chest

Opponent grasps the clothing at your chest with his left hand and attempts to set you up for a right-hand blow (Fig. 95).

Place your right hand over opponent's left hand and hold it tight to your chest. Grasp his wrist from underneath with your left hand (Fig. 96). Twist his arm until the back of his elbow is turned upward. At the same time, take a short step forward and across with your right foot while turning slightly to your left. While continuing to hold opponent's wrist with your left hand, place your right forearm over the back of his elbow so his elbow is in your armpit or under your biceps. Apply pressure downward by bending your trunk sideward and forward (Fig. 97). Counter with knee to chest area or follow up with the reverse wristlock and the thumb and forefinger come-along hold.

In using this technique, you should avoid the following common errors:

1. Pulling opponent's hand off your chest rather than holding it.
2. Grasping his wrist from the side with your right hand rather than

Figures 83 and 84. Counter to choke from front, arms extended—overhead throw using leg toss.

from underneath with his elbow close to your body. Grasping his wrist from the side diminishes your twisting ability considerably.

3. Bending your trunk too far forward when applying pressure to the back of the opponent's elbow. The trunk should be bent sideward and only slightly forward.

This technique may be followed up by an elbow smash, the reverse wrist-lock followed by the thumb and forefinger come-along hold, or by a bar hammerlock come-along hold.

Defense against Grasp on Chest—Wrist Throw

Opponent is standing in front of and facing you, grasps the clothing on your chest area and twists his hand clockwise. Step forward with your right foot and at the same time grasp opponent's right hand with your left hand. Place your thumb on the back of his hand, your thumb just below the knuckle of the middle finger and your fingers inside the point of his wrist. At the same time, grasp his hand with your right hand, placing your right thumb on the back of his hand below the knuckles. Quickly bend his wrist backward and toward him with both of your hands and a slight forward movement of your chest (Fig. 98). Twist his right hand counterclock-

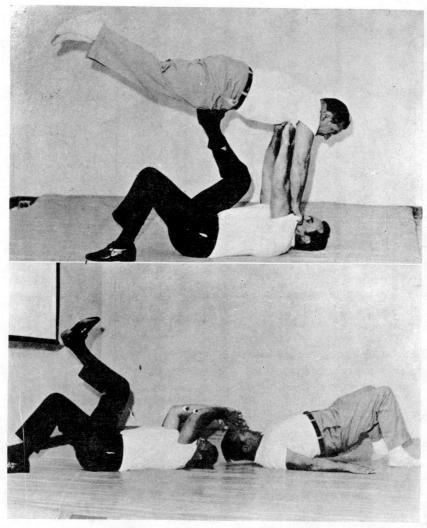

Figures 85 and 86. Overhead throw using leg toss.

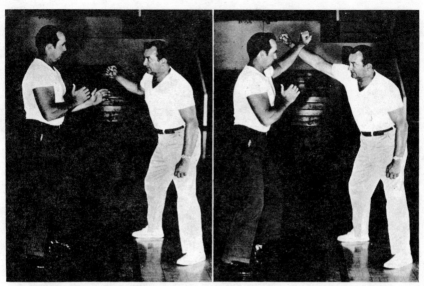

Figures 87 and 88. Defense against roundhouse punch to face—flying mare.

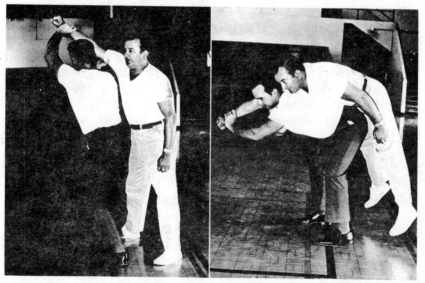

Figures 89 and 90. Flying mare.

Figure 91. Flying mare.

wise and downward about 45 degrees away from his body. Opponent is now leaning backwards and his weight shifts to his right leg (Fig. 99). As you apply pressure outward and downward with your right foot, step into the back of the knee joint of his right leg and throw opponent to his knees or to the ground for handcuffing procedure (Fig. 100).

Follow-ups you can use after taking opponent to the floor:

1. Apply your right knee on his rib cage or abdomen to prevent him from turning.

2. Pin his arm to the floor by placing your right knee on his biceps or elbow.

3. Keep pressure on his wrist, pull his arm up, twist and roll him over on his stomach; follow up with a reverse wristlock (Fig. 103).

Reverse Wristlock

Opponent is standing slightly to the left and facing you. Step forward with your left foot and at the same time grasp the opponent's left hand with your left hand. Place your thumb on the back of his hand, your thumb just below the knuckle of the middle finger and your fingers inside the palm of his hand; squeeze the muscle portion of the base of the little finger. Quickly bend his wrist and with a circular motion turn his hand backward

Figures 92 and 93. Counter to push on chest.

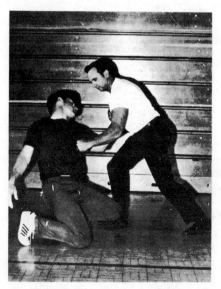

Figure 94. Counter to push on chest.

Figures 95 and 96. Counter to grasp on chest.

Figure 97. Counter to grasp on chest.

Figures 98 and 99. Counter to grasp on chest—wrist throw.

Figure 100. Wrist throw.

Figure 101. Reverse wristlock.

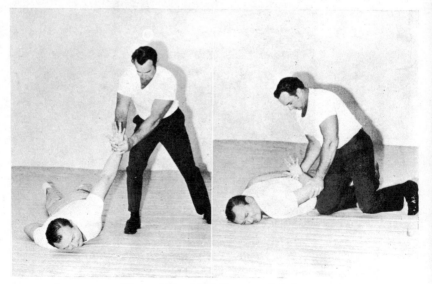

Figures 102 and 103. Reverse wristlock.

and upward towards himself. At the same time, grasp his hand with your right hand, and place your right thumb on the back of his hand below the knuckles with your fingers around the base of his thumb and in his palm close to the wrist. Raise his arm shoulder high (Fig. 101). Both thumbs should be high on the back of his hand just below his knuckles. Twist his wrist so that the palm of his hand is up. Bend his hand backward towards him—outward, counterclockwise and downward—so that the arm is about 45 degrees away from his body. Force the opponent to the floor (Fig. 102). As you apply the pressure outward and downward, step back with your left foot and take the opponent to the floor on his stomach. Move in behind the opponent as you carry and bend his left arm to the small of his back. Immediately bend his wrist back toward his elbow and continue the pressure. You may place your right knee on the small of his back to prevent opponent from turning over. The opponent is ready to be handcuffed (Fig. 103).

Chapter VII

DISARMING TECHNIQUES

Counter to a Knife Attack

Defending yourself against an opponent who attacks you with a knife is extremely dangerous. The first consideration should be to get out of his reach. Your second consideration should be to get your hands on something which will help you defend yourself. If you are not armed and are inside a room, such objects as a chair, a couch cushion or a table lamp are usually within reach. Outside, you may get a stick, a club, a brick or rock, a handful of dirt or sand. Some articles of your own clothing, such as your belt, a shoe or your coat could be used effectively.

The following techniques using your "personal weapons" should be used as a *last resort:*

Underhand and Upward Thrust. Opponent attacks with a knife, attempting an underhand and upward thrust. Step in with your right foot and block the thrust with the "V" formed by your hands by placing the right thumb over the left index finger and the left thumb under the right index and middle fingers. Your arms should be straight and elbows locked. Immediately grasp his wrist (Fig. 104). Raise his wrist sideward to your right and upward above his shoulder as you step under his arm with your left foot. Hold his wrist tight, arm straight, and twist over your head and on top of your right shoulder. Your back and buttocks should be braced against his waistline (Fig. 105). With a forward and downward pull on his arm, throw the opponent over your head and to the ground. *Note:* Holding his wrist tight, arm straight and the elbow on top of your right shoulder could cause injury to his arm, and force him to drop the knife.

Sideward Thrust. Opponent attacks with a knife attempting a sideward thrust. Step in with your right foot and block the thrust with the "V" formed by the hands, and immediately grasp his wrist (Fig. 106). Raise his arm over your head and to the right as you step across his body to your right with your left foot (Fig. 107). Carry his arm downward, twisting it clockwise so that his palm will be facing up as you bend at the hips sideways and bend your knees slightly. Pull him slightly forward so that the back of his elbow will be upward in front of your armpit and his upper arm will be up against your armpit (Fig. 108). The pressure is upward on the forearm and downward on his elbow. Force him to drop the knife by raising his forearm forcibly as you anchor his upper arm under your armpit, keeping

Figures 104 and 105. Knife—underhanded thrust.

your left elbow in tight, and continue twisting his hand clockwise as in a reverse wristlock (Fig. 109).

BACKHAND THRUST. Opponent attacks with a knife, attempting a backhand thrust. Step in with your right foot, block the thrust with the "V" formed by your hands and immediately grasp his wrist while still in backhand position (Fig. 110). Slide both of your hands to his wrist, place your thumbs on the back of his hand below his knuckles, bend his hand forward and downward and then twist it outward to your left (Fig. 111). As you apply pressure outward, step back with your left foot and take the opponent to the floor by twisting his hand downward toward the floor (Fig. 112). Follow up by placing your right knee to the rib cage or the abdomen.

COUNTER TO KNIFE OVERHEAD THRUST. Opponent attacks with a knife, attempting an overhead and a downward thrust. Step forward with your left foot and block the thrust close to the wrist in the overhead thrust position with the "V" formed with your hands. Your arms should be straight and elbows locked (Fig. 113). Immediately grasp his wrist with both hands. Your left hand is on his right wrist, your right arm underneath and around his upper arm. Grasp your left wrist with your right hand while pulling your right elbow in tight to your body, catching his upper arm in the crotch of your right elbow. Exert pressure backward and downward on his wrist,

Figures 106 and 107. Sideward thrust.

Figures 108 and 109. Sideward thrust.

Figures 110 and 111. Backhand thrust.

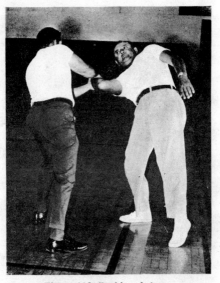

Figure 112. Backhand thrust.

and forward and upward on his upper arm and elbow. Step in with your right foot behind his right foot (Fig. 114). After bending opponent backward, step behind him with your right foot and take him to the floor over your right leg (Fig. 115).

Figures 113 and 114. Overhead thrust.

Figure 115. Overhead thrust.

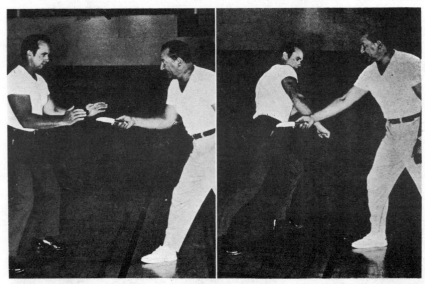

Figures 116 and 117. Straight-in thrust.

Figures 118 and 119. Straight-in thrust.

STRAIGHT-IN THRUST. Opponent attacks with a knife, attempting a straight-in thrust from the hip area. (This type of attack usually is an indication that the opponent is experienced in the use of a knife.) Protect your vital areas by keeping your hands up near your shoulders or face and your arms close to your body. Use your hands and arms to ward off a thrust, but do not reach out for the knife (Fig. 116). Endeavor to keep the opponent away from you by kicking with your front foot, returning quickly to a position of good balance. The opponent follows through with the straight-in thrust with the right hand. Quickly move your body to the left out of the line of thrust. With your outside right forearm, fist doubled, deliver a snap downward block to his outside right forearm, thus blocking the thrust (Fig. 117). Immediately follow up with a kick to the groin or lower abdomen (Fig. 118). Alternate block is to quickly move the body to the left out of the line of thrust, block the thrust with the "V" formed by the hands and immediately grasp his wrist (Fig. 119). Step across his body to the right with your left foot as you carry his arm downward, twisting it clockwise so that the palm of his hand faces up. Continue twisting his hand as in a reverse wristlock to force him to release the knife (Fig. 120).

Figure 120. Straight-in thrust.

Defense against a Handgun

Disarming an individual who is holding a knife or a gun is difficult and dangerous. In an emergency, knowledge of and skill in disarming techniques could well mean the difference between life and death. These techniques must be used in a *last resort* situation.

Points to remember for self-preservation:

1. When "covering" an opponent, do not bring your firearm "within reach" of your opponent's hands or feet.

2. Opponent should be placed in a disadvantageous position if it is necessary to bring the weapon "within reach."

3. Hold your weapon close to your body, elbow tight against your hip with your forearm parallel to the ground.

4. Approach opponent from the rear or side at a 45 to 90-degree angle. Approach should be made by two or more officers. Keep your opponent at the apex of a triangle.

5. Be constantly alert for any movement of the hands, arms, feet or trunk, or of a shifting of the eyes which indicates his intentions to disarm you or do you harm.

6. Do not permit your opponent to distract you by talking, moving about or allowing any favors.

7. Select and execute an effective technique that is simple and practical in bringing your opponent under control in a particular situation.

8. The most important procedure of an "effective technique" is to get your body out of the line of fire, then to gain and maintain control of the gun throughout the maneuver, followed by possession of the gun, and finally to bring the subject under complete physical control in a reasonably short time.

9. *Know your gun.*

10. Judgment is of utmost importance in knowing how and when to disarm. The gun must be "within reach." Generally, do not attempt to disarm until you have exhausted all other possibilities and have reason to believe you are going to be shot. Attempt to disarm only as a *last resort*.

Disarming from the Front, Hands-up Position

Before attempting to disarm an opponent of his gun, the weapon must be within easy reach. Disarming must be an absolute necessity. Talk to the opponent to keep him engrossed and off guard. Obey his commands to "get your hands up" and raise your hands to approximately shoulder height (Fig. 121). The first and most important movement is to get your body out of the line of fire, then to gain control of the gun and disarm the opponent.

RAKE ACROSS FACE. Twist the body out of the line of fire. Because the twisting movement is mostly in the hips and knees, this takes the body out of the line of fire. This is the first and most important movement and precedes practically all disarming techniques from the front and the back. This preliminary movement consists of making contact with the gun with either

Figures 121 and 122. Gun—front, rake across face.

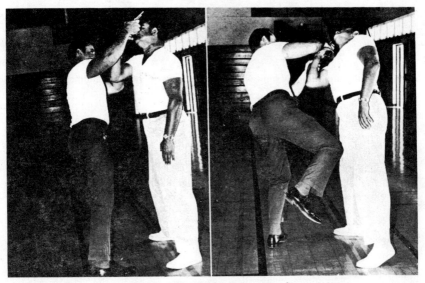

Figures 123 and 124. Rake across face.

hand, preferably over the cylinder, with the knuckles up and the thumb under the barrel (Fig. 122). With the right foot, step forward towards your opponent and at the same time place your right hand under the barrel or trigger guard, palm up. Grasp firmly and bend the wrist and the muzzle of the gun directly towards your opponent. Continue twisting the gun and the wrist counterclockwise, hitting the opponent across the face with the barrel (Fig. 123). At the same time, lift your right knee into opponent's groin or stomach area (Fig. 124). Control your hold on the gun, twisting the gun out of his hand while in the wrist-throw position (Fig. 125).

Figure 125. Rake across face.

FINGER BREAK. Start from a half "hands up" position. The feet are slightly spread, your weight on the balls of the feet, knees are slightly bent, and your eyes are focused on subject's face (Fig. 126).

As a general rule, "go for the gun with the hand that is closest to the weapon."

Twist to the left and move your body out of line of fire. Using your right hand and making contact over the cylinder of the gun. Carry the gun just off the body to your left (Fig. 127).

Start forcing the barrel toward the opponent and twisting the gun clockwise. With the left hand, thumb up, make contact with the gun as close to the barrel as possible. When the barrel of the gun reaches a vertical posi-

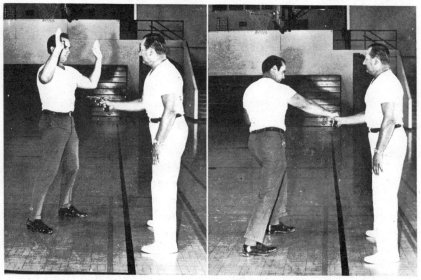

Figures 126 and 127. Front, finger break.

Figures 128 and 129. Finger break.

tion, apply pressure directly backward so that the barrel of the gun is pointing toward the opponent. The opponent's trigger finger is caught in the trigger guard (Fig. 128).

The trigger finger is locked in the trigger guard. Pull the gun downward and to the right side of your body. The barrel pointing in the direction of your right foot (Fig. 129).

Disarming from the Front, Hands-down Position—Scissors of Both Hands

A gun is placed in your abdomen and you are commanded to put your hands up (Fig. 130). Looking straight into suspect's eyes, start the initial movement, both hands reaching a point several inches below the gun. The right hand goes to the inside of your opponent's wrist and at the same time, the left hand makes contact with the barrel of the gun close to the cylinder; the thumbs are up (Fig. 131). The heel of the right hand hits hard at the break of the wrist and the fingers close around the wrist. The left hand pushes the barrel of the gun sideward under your right forearm, then downward and inward until the muzzle points under the assailant's right arm (Fig. 132). Complete the movement by jerking the wrist toward you and pushing the gun in the opposite direction (Fig. 133). Follow up with a kick to the groin (Fig. 134).

Disarming from the Rear, Hands-up Position—Gun Low

Opponent places a gun into the small of your back (gun low). Glance over your shoulder to determine which hand is holding the gun (Fig. 135). Turn to your left or to his inside right elbow, pivoting on your right foot and moving the left foot a step back. Your left arm remains bent, your elbow passes over the opponent's forearm and traps it as close to the wrist as possible between your left arm and body. The left hand should grasp the opponent's arm just above the elbow and your arm should be under his forearm, catching his wrist in the crook of your elbow. When pivot is completed, your left foot should be slightly outside of the opponent's right foot and you should be facing him at about a 45-degree angle, with feet comfortably spread and knees slighlty bent (Fig. 136). Lifting his elbow upward, follow up immediately with blow by the heel of the right hand to the chin or to some other vulnerable spot, and a right kneelift to the groin (Fig. 137). If opponent attempts to jerk the gun from under your arm, do not resist but go with him, making it impossible for him to dislodge the gun. Do not release the gun from under your arm until the opponent is definitely under control. After the initial blow has been struck, you can follow up further by bringing your right leg outside and behind the subject's right leg, placing your right foot behind and inside subject's right foot and striking a heel-of-hand blow and push to the chin. The opponent will be forced to the floor

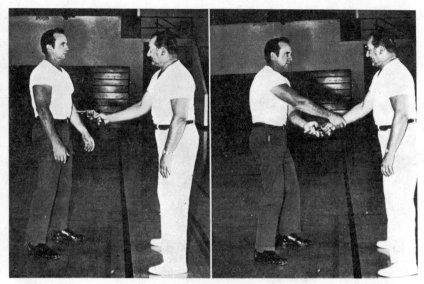

Figures 130 and 131. Front, scissors.

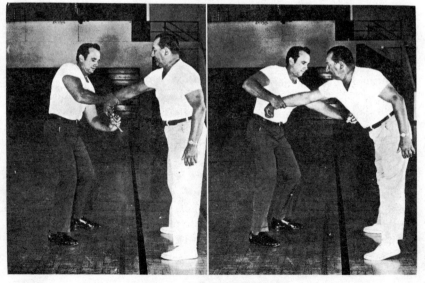

Figures 132 and 133. Scissors.

Figure 134. Scissors.

and his right forearm will remain trapped under your left arm. Pressure can be applied with your knee to the back of his elbow, to the rib cage or side of the body.

Disarming from the Rear, Hands-up Position—Gun High

Opponent places gun in your back. Glance over your shoulder to determine which hand is holding the gun (Fig. 138). Twist your body toward his outside elbow and bring your right arm downward and under his right elbow (like windmill action); as you turn to the right, pivot on the right heel and move the left foot to the right side. The arm should straighten out and you should strike opponent's forearm or wrist with your right hand or forearm (Fig. 139). Contact is then made with the left hand on your opponent's forearm, thus controlling the gun hand (Fig. 140). Right hand then grasps the gun under the barrel close to the cylinder, palm up, as the left hand slips down the forearm to the wrist. The muzzle is forced inward and upward toward opponent's left shoulder, and raked across the face. At the same time, the gun is twisted counterclockwise with wrist-break technique (Fig. 141). Disarm, step back and point weapon at the opponent (Fig. 142).

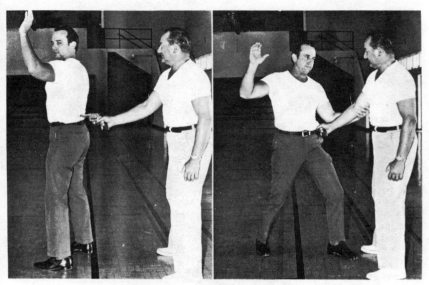

Figures 135 and 136. Rear, gun low.

Figure 137. Rear, gun low.

Figures 138 and 139, Rear, gun high.

Figures 140 and 141. Rear, gun high.

Figure 142. Rear, gun high.

Chapter VIII

IN OR OUT OF AUTOMOBILE

FREQUENTLY, the opponent refuses to get out of a car or refuses to be placed into a car. There are several techniques which can be used in these situations.

Taking Opponent Out of a Car

The approach to the driver of the vehicle is made from the left rear. Always keep your eyes on the hands of the driver except for a brief glance into the rear seat of the car to be sure no one is on the floor of the car. Do not go forward of the doorpost on the driver's side, in order to prevent the opponent from suddenly opening the car door and throwing you off balance or knocking you to the ground. Approach an open door with the left or right foot first at about a 45-degree angle so as to prevent a blow to your groin. Always be in command of the situation.

REVERSE WRISTLOCK AND THUMB AND FOREFINGER COME-ALONG HOLD. Step in with your right or left foot towards the driver, protecting yourself from a blow to the groin. Grasp the opponent's left arm above the elbow with your right hand (Fig. 143). Grasp opponent's left wrist, placing your thumb underneath the break of his wrist. Your fingers are on top of the back of his hand and below the knuckles. Immediately pull his arm free from the steering wheel, move it backward with his elbow against the doorpost of the car (Fig. 144), and twist the arm so that the palm faces up (Fig. 145). Now apply a reverse wristlock and remove him from the car with the thumb and forefinger come-along hold (Fig. 146).

BAR HAMMERLOCK COME-ALONG. Step in with your right or left foot towards the driver, protecting yourself from a blow to the groin. Grasp the opponent's left arm above the elbow with your right hand. Grasp the opponent's left wrist with your left hand. Opponent resists and will not leave his grasp on the steering wheel. With the heel of your right arm, lift his left elbow upward and immediately force his left hand downward and backward, causing his elbow to bend (Fig. 147). Move behind him as you place his left wrist in the crotch of your right elbow and move it toward his left shoulder. To maintain better control, lift your elbow upward as you exert pressure downward on his elbow with your left hand (Fig. 148). Remove opponent slowly from car, allowing him to maneuver legs outward and out of car.

79

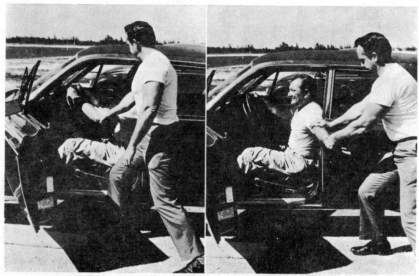

Figures 143 and 144. Out of car—reverse wristlock, thumb and forefinger come-along.

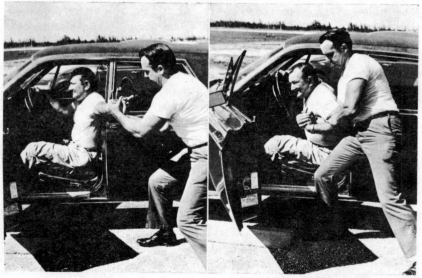

Figures 145 and 146. Reverse wristlock, thumb and forefinger come-along.

HEAD TWIST WITH MASTOID PRESSURE POINT. Step in with your right foot so as to protect yourself against a hand blow to the groin. When the opponent attempts to lean away from you, use the heel of your left hand to push the opponent's head and face to the right. Immediately reach around behind his head with your right hand, grasp his chin in your cupped hand and twist his neck to the right and backward. Additional leverage to this twisting action may be obtained by using his right shoulder as the fulcrum for your right forearm. Now place the tip of your left thumb into his left mastoid and apply pressure inward and upward (Fig. 149). Continue twisting his neck clockwise and applying pressure to his left mastoid as you take him out of the car (Fig. 150).

Placing Opponent Into a Car

FINGERLOCK COME-ALONG. (This hold is particularly useful for escorting females for short distances and for placing individuals into a car.) Opponent grasps the upper window frame of the car door. Step forward with your closest leg first and at the same time, grasp the opponent's right upper arm above the elbow with your left hand. With your right hand, grasp the opponent's right hand by taking hold of the small finger or the two middle fingers (Fig. 151). Bend the fingers backward, with his palm facing upward. Continue the forward pressure of your left hand while the opponent's fingers are being bent backward, causing him to walk on his toes. The forearm is parallel to the ground (Fig. 152). Now have the opponent work his way into the car as pressure is applied.

An alternate method may be used at this point. Grasp and place his right elbow between your left arm and left rib cage and continue backward pressure on his fingers. Slide your left arm forward and grasp the two middle fingers with your left hand, thus releasing your right hand to open car door or to handcuff (Fig. 153).

BAR HAMMERLOCK COME-ALONG. Opponent grasps upper car door window frame. Approach opponent by placing your closest leg forward to prevent a blow to your groin area; at the same time, grasp his upper right arm with your left hand above the elbow (Fig. 154). With your right hand, grasp the opponent's right wrist and with your left hand lift upward on his right elbow joint (Fig. 155), pulling downward on the right wrist and rotating his right forearm clockwise (Fig. 156). This action brings the opponent's right wrist into the bend of your left arm. From this position, press the opponent's right elbow downward and lift his right forearm upward against his back. This action will cause the opponent to lean forward and into the car. To bring the opponent to the upright position so that he may walk, grasp his opposite shoulder, his hair or his head with your right hand (Fig. 157).

Figures 147 and 148. Out of car—bar hammerlock come-along.

Figures 149 and 150. Out of car—head twist with mastoid pressure point.

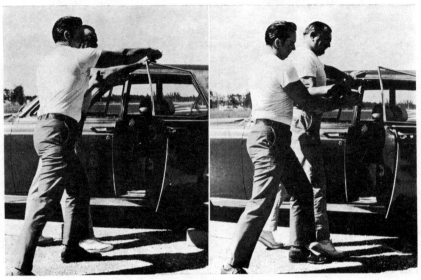

Figures 151 and 152. Into car—fingerlock come-along.

Figure 153. Fingerlock come-along.

Figures 154 and 155. Into car—bar hammerlock come-along.

Figures 156 and 157. Bar hammerlock come-along.

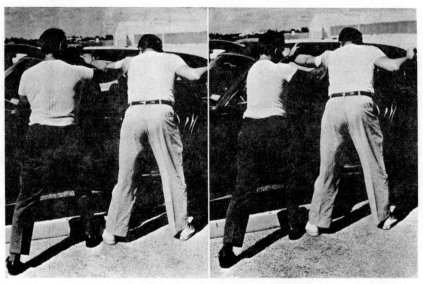

Figures 158 and 159. Into car—arms between legs come-along.

Figure 160. Arms between legs come-along.

ARM BETWEEN THE LEGS COME-ALONG. Opponent resists going into a car by placing one hand on top of the roof of the car and one hand on top of car door. Approach with your nearest leg first and at the same time, with your right hand, apply forward pressure on opponent's left shoulder (Fig. 158). Suddenly, release the pressure on his left shoulder and with your left hand, deliver a blow to his left wrist (Fig. 159). Pull his left arm downward and pass it between his legs from the front. Reach down with your right hand, grasp his left wrist from behind him and pull it backward and upward. Push on the back of his neck or collar with your left hand to help bend his upper body downward (Fig. 160). The opponent is completely off balance and can easily be maneuvered into the car.

ORDER FORM

CUSTOM PUBLISHING COMPANY

P.O. BOX 22986, SACRAMENTO, CA 95822

Order Today!

Your Name _____

Title _____ Agency _____

Address _____

City _____ State _____ Zip _____

Total Amount Enclosed $ _____ (CA orders add 6%)

Add $1.00 for first book and 50¢ for each additional book to cover postage and handling

AGENCY PURCHASE ORDERS: (only accepted for orders over $40.00)

Prices Subject to Change

ALL ORDERS MUST BE PREPAID EXCEPT AS STATED

Contact us for quantity discount schedule

____ ea. Community Relations Concepts $17.95
____ ea. Courtroom Survival $9.95
____ ea. Criminal Interrogation $12.95
____ ea. Fingerprint Science $12.95
____ ea. New Police Report Manual $9.95
____ ea. Officer Survival Manual $11.95
____ ea. PC 832 Concepts II $12.95
____ ea. Police Unarmed Defense Tactics $7.95
____ ea. Practical Criminal Investigation $19.95
____ ea. Prin. of Amer. Law Enf. & Crim. Just $24.95
____ ea. Search and Seizure Handbook $11.95
____ ea. Traffic Investigation and Enforcement $17.95
____ ea. Understanding Street Gangs $12.95
____ ea. **SPECIAL RUTLEDGE "5- PAK" $44.95**

PROUDLY SERVING LAW ENFORCEMENT SINCE 1969
Your Partner in Education